PICTURE LIBRARY

GERBILS

PICTURE LIBRARY
GERBILS

Norman Barrett

Franklin Watts

London   New York   Sydney   Toronto

©1990 Franklin Watts Ltd

First published in Great Britain
1990 by
Franklin Watts Ltd
96 Leonard Street
London EC2A 4RH

First published in the United States by
Franklin Watts Inc
387 Park Avenue South
New York
NY 10016

First published in Australia by
Franklin Watts
14 Mars Road
Lane Cove
NSW 2066

UK ISBN: 0 7496 0106 X

A CIP catalogue record for
this book is available from
the British Library

Printed in Italy

Designed by
Barrett & Weintroub

Photographs by
Marc Henrie
Pat Morris
Survival Anglia
Anthony Bannister/NHPA
Sally Anne Thompson
Smithsonian Institution

Illustration by
Rhoda & Robert Burns

Technical Consultant
David Alderton

Contents

Introduction

Gerbils are small, furry, ratlike animals. They make ideal pets – lively, gentle and easy to care for. In the wild, they live in dry regions of Africa and Asia.

△ The wild gerbil is usually brownish black in colour, with a pale underside. It lives in desert areas.

There are about 80 species (kinds) of wild gerbil. Most have long hind legs and a long, furry tail. They are members of the rodent family. But they are more closely related to hamsters and voles than to rats.

Nearly all the gerbils bred as pets are Mongolian gerbils. They come originally from Mongolia, a desert area between northern China and the Soviet Union.

These gerbils are about 10 cm (4 in) long from nose to tail, and the tail is as long again as the body. They use their hind legs to travel in huge leaps and bounds, but they also walk and run on all fours.

△ Gerbils are gentle creatures and make excellent pets.

Looking at gerbils

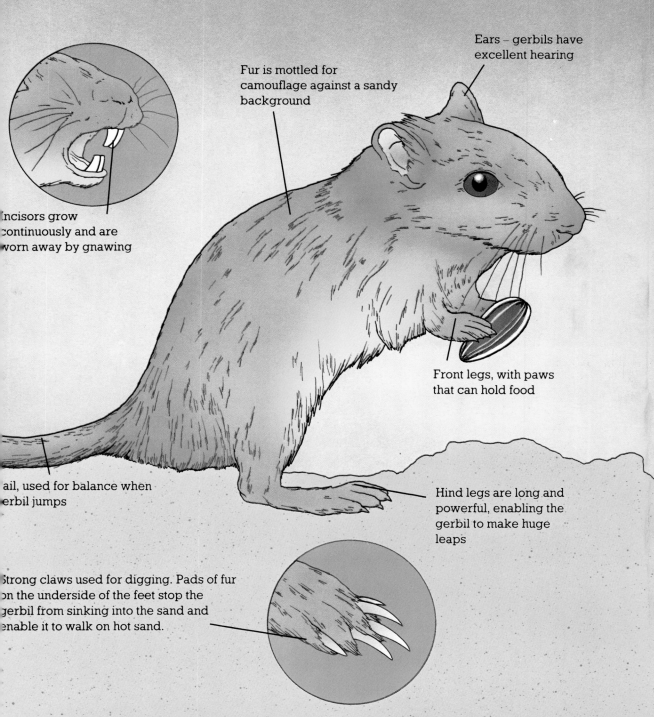

Incisors grow continuously and are worn away by gnawing

Fur is mottled for camouflage against a sandy background

Ears – gerbils have excellent hearing

Front legs, with paws that can hold food

Tail, used for balance when gerbil jumps

Hind legs are long and powerful, enabling the gerbil to make huge leaps

Strong claws used for digging. Pads of fur on the underside of the feet stop the gerbil from sinking into the sand and enable it to walk on hot sand.

Where they come from

Gerbils and their close relatives are found throughout the desert areas of Africa and Asia. The pet gerbil originally comes from Mongolia.

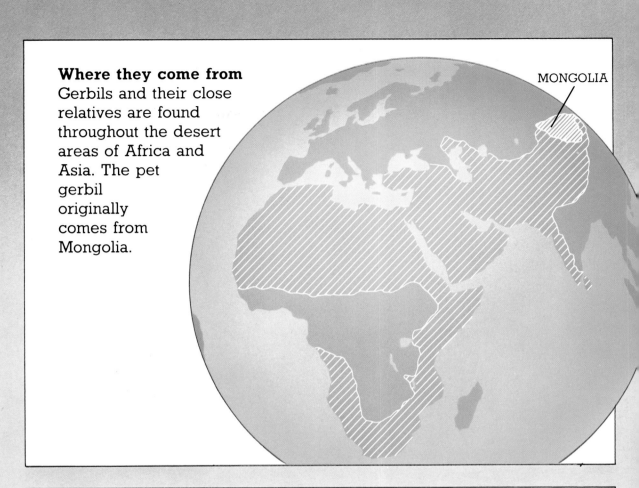

MONGOLIA

Tunnelling gerbils

Gerbils are fast and efficient tunnellers. They use their sharp front claws to dig into the soil and their powerful hind feet to kick away debris. They often dig their burrows near clumps of plants, where roots hold the soil together. Gerbils make a nesting room, which they line first with chewed grass or seeds and then with whole leaves. They make food storage rooms to fill during the spring and summer.

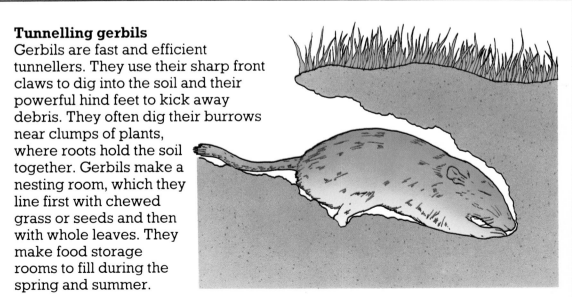

Living in the desert

In the wild, gerbils stay in their burrows during the hottest part of the day. They come out in the evening and are most active around midnight.

The gerbil's long, bounding jump helps to keep its feet from too much contact with the hot ground. The soles of its feet are covered with a furry pad. This also protects it from the hot ground and prevents its feet from sinking into soft sand.

△ A gerbil comes out of its burrow in the sand dunes of the desert. Its so-called agouti colouring provides excellent camouflage against the sandy background.

Gerbils live in groups or colonies. Each gerbil family inhabits a complex of burrows with as many as six or seven entrances and a main tunnel up to 4 m (13 ft) long.

They stay close to their burrows, rarely venturing more than about 15 m (50 ft) away. They use their powerful hind legs to bound away from their enemies, such as foxes, snakes and birds, and escape to their burrow.

▽ A gerbil in its burrow, as seen through glass. Gerbils dig their burrows down to one metre (3 ft) or more.

◁ A gerbil eating seeds on the sands of the Namib desert, in south-western Africa.

Wild gerbils feed on seeds, leaves, roots and other plant matter. They need very little water because they can store moisture extracted from food in their body fat. Their kidneys do not produce a lot of urine, which is why pet gerbils do not have smelly cages.

In the winter, when they become less active, wild gerbils use stocks of food stored during the spring and summer months.

Gerbils do not gather in large groups. They prefer to live with their own family. They are prepared to fight off other gerbils who intrude on their territory or threaten them in any way.

Gerbils make very little sound. Young gerbils may squeak in their nest, but adults squeak only when frightened. They distinguish members of their family from outsiders chiefly by smell.

▽ Gerbils identify members of their own family by smell. The males mark their territory and each other with scent from a gland in their abdomen (belly).

Birth and growing up

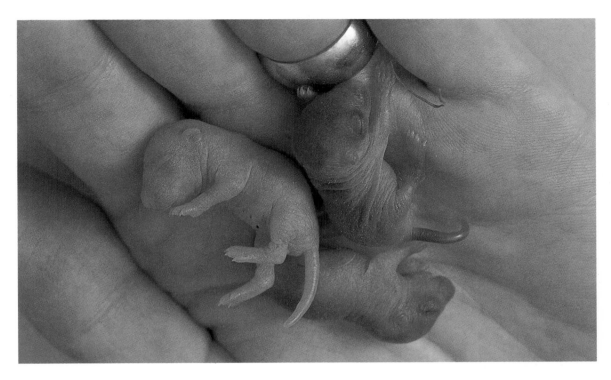

Female gerbils have from 1 to 12 young, although litters average about 4 or 5. At birth, the baby gerbils are blind, deaf, toothless and without fur.

The young mature quickly, and at about 12 weeks can have babies themselves. In the wild, the young adults leave their burrow to find mates and set up their own homes.

Domestic gerbils rarely live for more than five years. In the wild, their life span is even shorter.

△ One-day-old gerbils in a person's hand. They are completely naked and blind, but they soon begin to see and grow a coat of soft fur. They are weaned off their mother's milk in 3 or 4 weeks.

◁Young gerbils become adults very quickly. They reach adolescence at about nine weeks and can mate and start a family of their own after 12. In the wild, young gerbils travel no more than a few metres to set up a new home, perhaps in a disused burrow. With enemies such as snakes and owls around, many do not survive.

Kinds of gerbils

In addition to the familiar Mongolian gerbil, species of wild gerbils include pygmy gerbils, short-tailed or bushy-tailed gerbils and hairy-footed gerbils.

The colour of wild gerbils usually blends in with their rocky or sandy surroundings. It is mostly reddish brown, but may range from yellow to dark grey. Gerbils within the same species may differ in colour.

△ A pair of wild Mongolian gerbils. These are also called clawed jirds.

▷ A pet Mongolian gerbil.

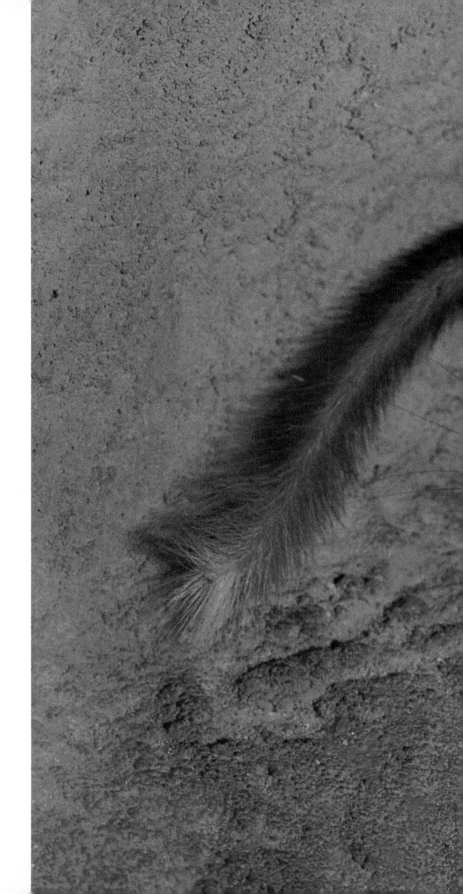

▷ The bushy-tailed jird, as its name suggests, is notable for its bushy tail. It lives in the Middle East, from eastern Egypt and southern Israel to central Arabia.

Mongolian gerbils have been bred as pets in a variety of colours, from black to pure white. They are all the same species of gerbil, and grow to a similar size and have similar features and habits. Only the colour varies.

△ Gerbils in a range of familiar coats. These are known as (from the top): argente, black, agouti and dove.

▷ A white gerbil with pink eyes.

▽ A grey agouti gerbil. The term agouti refers to the type of colouring rather than the colour itself. Agouti hairs are paler at the base, with darker tips. Wild gerbils have agouti colouring.

△Special terms are used by breeders to describe gerbil colouring. They are not always obviously descriptive, as in the "blue" gerbil above.

◁A black patched gerbil.

▷An argente gerbil.

Keeping gerbils

Gerbils make such good pets because they are clean and easy to look after, and they do not smell. They are lively and curious creatures, but are easy to tame and rarely bite.

A gerbil's cage should have a floor covering of wood shavings (not sawdust) or some other material such as peat that they can burrow in. Hay is good for sleeping on, or you can buy a special bedding material.

▽ The floor of a gerbil's home with the cage removed. There are separate containers for food and water, and some simple "toys" such as a piece of wood for gnawing on. Gerbils prefer a thicker floor covering than this, because they enjoy burrowing. Fish tanks may be converted to make good housing for gerbils.

Gerbils like company, so it is best to keep two. Their cage, or gerbilarium, might have two or three floors for extra exercise space.

Gerbils need feeding once a day. Pet shops sell a mixture of maize, oats and pelleted food. They also enjoy raw vegetables and fruit, and love sunflower seeds as a treat. They need little water, but it must be kept clean. You can buy special bottles to fix to their cage, which they learn to drink from.

△ Gerbils sleep for short periods and are active both day and night. They may be handled when they have become tame and are used to people. They should be well supported, and held gently but firmly. Care must be taken not to touch the tip of the tail, which is easily injured.

The story of gerbils

Surviving in the desert

Gerbils have developed over many thousands of years to live safely in the harsh conditions of the deserts of Africa and Asia. In some parts of the world, small rodents that look like gerbils have developed in very similar ways in desert habitats, although they are not related directly to the gerbil. These include the jerboas, which live in Asia, the Australian hopping mouse and the North American kangaroo rat.

△ Jerboas are not close relatives of gerbils, but they are similar in appearance and habits.

Discovering gerbils

In 1866, a French missionary and naturalist called Père David was the first European to discover gerbils and write about them. He sent back dead specimens of Mongolian gerbils from China to the Paris Museum of Natural History.

△ French missionary Père David, who discovered gerbils in Asia.

Gerbils in captivity

All the pet gerbils in the world are descendants of 20 pairs of gerbils captured in eastern Mongolia in 1935. These were sent to Tokyo, and used as a basis for breeding the species in a laboratory.

In 1954, 11 pairs of this breeding group were sent to the United States for use in scientific research. They were successfully bred and, within ten years, thousands of Mongolian gerbils had been produced from this small colony. The scientists working with them found them to be gentle animals, and they became popular pets. Their popularity also spread to Europe.

Gerbils and science
Scientists found that gerbils were ideal laboratory animals. Some people feel that it is wrong to use animals in this way. But gerbils have been extremely helpful to scientists researching into dangerous illnesses such as heart disease, cancer and epilepsy.

Gerbils are also useful to scientists studying the problems of long space flights. Scientists are interested in the gerbil's control of its body temperature, its ability to make water out of dry food, and its high resistance to radiation.

Breeding
Several variations in coat colour from the natural, wild colouring have appeared in tame gerbils, even white. This would reduce the gerbil's chance of survival in the wild – its white coat would make it conspicuous to predators. But in captivity, such animals do not face the dangers of the wild. Animals accidentally born with the same unusual features can be mated, and this is how black,

grey, lilac and white gerbils have all been bred.

△ A white gerbil, bred as a pet, would not survive in the wild. The natural colouring of wild gerbils helps them to blend in with their surroundings.

Shows
The National Mongolian Gerbil Society was founded in England in 1968. It sets the standards to which gerbils are exhibited, based on an agreed idea of the "perfect" gerbil. The gerbil is shown in a special, small show pen with a wire front, in which it can be seen clearly and easily removed.

Judges award points for such features as colour, fur, eyes and ears and for condition and size. They deduct points if the gerbil is too fat, is moulting or has stained fur and if the show pen is dirty.

Facts and records

△ The body of the tassel-tailed pygmy gerbil, which lives in the Namib desert, measures only about 5 cm (2 in), but its tail is very much longer.

Size
Wild gerbils range in size from about 5 to 25 cm (2–10 in). The smallest gerbils are the various species of pygmy gerbils, and the largest is the great gerbil, which lives in the deserts of south-western Asia.

Storing food
Some wild gerbils store more food than they will need in winter.

The great gerbil might store as much as 50 kg (110 lb). Gerbils can cause problems in some farming areas by overstoring, as they raid the sparse crops for their supplies.

Survival
Only about one in five gerbil babies survive in the wild. The rest are taken by predators. But females, who carry their young in their body for only 24 to 26 days, can have up to four litters a year. So predators are no threat to the survival of wild gerbil species.

Glossary

Adolescence
The stage of life between baby and adult.

Agouti
A type of coat colouring in which the hairs vary in colour along their length. Wild gerbils have agouti coats.

Argente
The golden brown colouring of some varieties of pet gerbil.

Camouflage
Colouring that helps an animal to blend in with its surroundings, making it hard to be spotted by its enemies.

Gerbilarium
A special glass or plastic tank built as a home for pet gerbils. The best gerbilariums have a deep floor covering and other stages so that the gerbils can exercise and play.

Habitat
The type of area where a particular animal lives in the wild.

Incisors
Front teeth used for cutting and gnawing. These grow continually, and become too long if the gerbil does not get enough hard things to chew on. They may be clipped by a vet.

Jird
Another name for the gerbil.

Litter
The babies born at one time. The average litter is four or five baby gerbils.

Moulting
Shedding hair.

Naturalist
A person who studies wildlife.

Pelleted food
A specially prepared food, in the form of pellets, containing all the necessary ingredients, including vitamins and minerals, to keep a pet in top condition.

Predator
An animal that preys on another, killing it for food.

Weaned
Eating solid food, having stopped depending on a mother's milk.

Index